t's Eyes to Reflectors

Tech from Nature

By Jennifer Colby

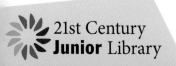

21st Century
Junior Library

Published in the United States of America by
Cherry Lake Publishing
Ann Arbor, Michigan
www.cherrylakepublishing.com

Reading Adviser: Marla Conn, MS, Ed., Literacy specialist, Read-Ability, Inc.
Content Adviser: Rachel Brown, MA, Sustainable Business

Library of Congress Cataloging-in-Publication Data

Names: Colby, Jennifer, 1971– author.
Title: Cat's eyes to reflectors / Jennifer Colby.
Description: Ann Arbor : Cherry Lake Publishing, [2019] | Series: Tech from nature | Audience: Grade 4 to 6. |
    Includes bibliographical references and index.
Identifiers: LCCN 2018035193 | ISBN 9781534142916 (hardcover) | ISBN 9781534140677 (pdf) |
    ISBN 9781534139473 (pbk.) | ISBN 9781534141872 (hosted ebook)
Subjects: LCSH: Reflectors (Safety devices)—Juvenile literature. | Biomimicry—Juvenile literature.
Classification: LCC TE228 .C65 2019 | DDC 625.7/94—dc23
LC record available at https://lccn.loc.gov/2018035193

Cherry Lake Publishing would like to acknowledge the work of the Partnership for 21st Century Skills.
Please visit *www.p21.org* for more information.

Printed in the United States of America
Corporate Graphics

CONTENTS

Driving in bad weather or at night can be dangerous.

Driving Through the Darkness

Have you ever ridden in a car at night? It is hard to see the road! Is it rainy, snowing, or foggy? These conditions make driving in the dark even more dangerous.

Streetlights light the way at night.

Road Safety Throughout the Years

For thousands of years, roads have been built for people to travel on. Oil, gas, and electric lights have **illuminated** busy roads.

Lights became more common on roads. But there were still long **stretches** of road that had no lighting. Streetlights were expensive. They were only located in busy city areas. Country roads were dark and dangerous to travel on.

Headlights help drivers see at night.

Cars became more widely used in the early 1900s. Accidents on dark roads also became more common. Electric headlights on cars were first introduced in 1898. But something else was needed to help drivers **navigate** through the darkness. A simple answer was found in the most unexpected place—cats! Let's find out more.

Look!

Next time you ride in a car at night, look for streetlights. Do you have any streetlights around where you live?

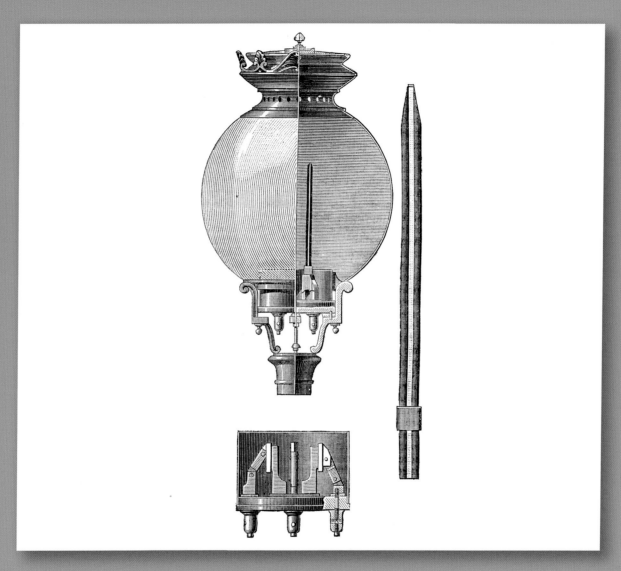

Electric streetlights used to be called "electric candles."

A Light in the Night

Percy Shaw made his living building and maintaining roads. He lived in England in the 1930s. He was always nervous driving home on dark and foggy nights. There were no streetlights to light his way. There were no markings on the road. It was hard to see where the road started and ended. He could have easily driven off the road!

Have you ever seen a cat's eyes glowing at night?

Shaw's headlights passed over the eyes of a stray cat. The light that **reflected** back gave Shaw his idea! What if he could make something that reflected like a cat's eye on the road? It would help mark the road at night.

Shaw spent the rest of his life working on this. He developed, manufactured, and improved the Catseye Reflecting Roadstud. It consisted of a pair of reflective glass "eyes" in a protective **housing**.

Cars can drive over a roadstud without damaging it or the car.

These early roadstuds were put into the middle of a road at regular **intervals**. Because of their **durable** construction, one roadstud could last for many years.

Think!

What other types of road safety devices help make travel safer? Write down what you can think of. Then ask an adult for help to identify more devices that make roads safer. Do you think any of these devices were inspired by animals or nature?

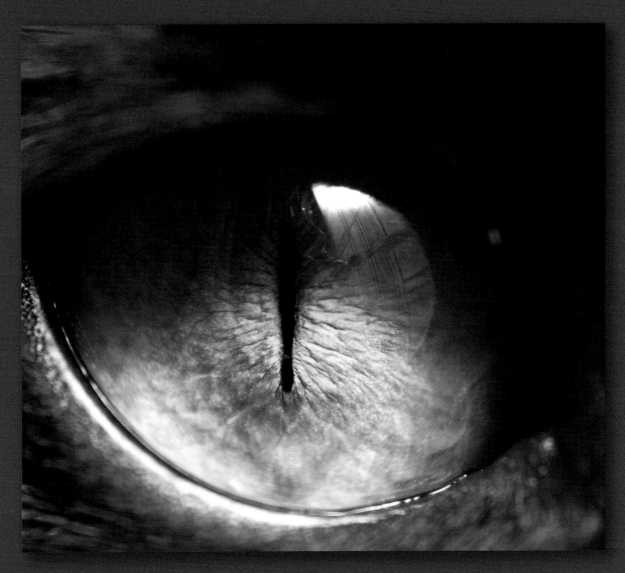

Cat's eyes contain a reflective tissue.

Investigating Nature

Shaw's invention was based on the concept of **biomimicry**. It is a rapidly growing scientific field of research.

The glass eyes of the roadstud are similar to a cat's eyes. Cats have a layer of tissue at the back of their eyes called tapetum lucidum. This tissue reflects the light that enters their eyes. It creates more light for the cat to use when it is trying to see.

Eyeshine occurs in animals of all kinds.

Their eyes absorb all the available light and then send it back out. This is how cats can see in the dark!

This characteristic is called **eyeshine**. It is what makes a cat's eyes look like they're glowing in the dark. Dogs, raccoons, cows, sheep, many fish, and some birds also have this tissue in their eyes.

Make a Guess!

Why do you think some animals have reflective tissue in their eyes and others don't? Use the internet and resources at your library to find out!

Reflectors on bicycles make them more visible.

Road travel became safer thanks to this discovery. Reflective items are now used for many other purposes. Bicycles have reflectors on them. Clothes have reflective material. These reflective features make everyone safer.

Ask Questions!

What other features of animals are unique? Visit the zoo and pick an animal to observe. Take notes. Then, ask a librarian to help you find out more about the animal. Maybe you'll be inspired to invent something!

GLOSSARY

biomimicry (bye-oh-MIM-ik-ree) copying plants and animals to build or improve something

durable (DOOR-uh-buhl) staying strong and in good condition for a long time

eyeshine (EYE-shine) a glow of reflected light that appears in the eyes of animals

housing (HOUZ-ing) something that covers or protects something else

illuminated (ih-LOO-muh-nayt-id) shined light on

intervals (IN-ter-vuhlz) amounts of space in between

navigate (NAV-ih-gayt) to find the way to get to a place when you are traveling

reflected (rih-FLEKT-id) gave back light

stretches (STRECH-ez) continuous lengths

FIND OUT MORE

BOOKS

Duprat, Guillaume. *EYE SPY: Wild Ways Animals See the World.* Smyrna, TN: What on Earth Publishing, 2018.

La Bella, Laura. *A Career in Paving and Road Surfacing.* New York: Rosen Young Adult, 2018.

WEBSITES

Inventive Kids
http://inventivekids.com
Learn about inventors, inventions, and how you can become an inventor.

Paws—About Cats
https://www.paws.org/kids/learn/pets/cats
Discover many facts about cats and how to take care of them.

INDEX

ABOUT THE AUTHOR

Jennifer Colby is a school librarian in Ann Arbor, Michigan. She loves reading, traveling, and going to museums to learn about new things.